TAMING
YOUR
INNER
SUPERVISOR

BOOK
FOUR

WHY
PROJECTS
FAIL

haag press

by Ruth Haag

illustrated by Bob Haag

TAMING YOUR INNER SUPERVISOR   BOOK FOUR   WHY PROJECTS FAIL

Text and illustrations Copyright © 2001 by Ruth S. Haag

Published by haag press

Printed in the United States of America
For information contact: Haag Press, 1064 N. Main St. #401,
Bowling Green, OH 43402-1346

Library of Congress Control Number: 2001130007

ISBN 0-9665497-6-7

Excerpted quotes reprinted with permission of Simon & Schuster from PEOPLE OF THE LIE by M. Scott Peck, M.D. Copyright © 1983 by M. Scott Peck, M.D.

to Bob

redefining the world
with me,
every day

Other books by Ruth Haag

Taming Your Inner Supervisor
Day to Day Supervising
Hiring and Firing
The Executive's Summary™

Old Married Friends'™ Advice

The Cookbook to English Dictionary
The Useable Cookbook: Main Dishes
The Useable Cookbook: Desserts
The Useable Cookbook: Breads, Spreads, and Veggies

TABLE OF CONTENTS

PROLOG: Supervising Styles Vary in Predictable Ways

When people make decisions, they think about three separate items to varying degrees: themselves, other people and the thing to be accomplished. Many people make lop-sided decisions by putting too much, or all, of their emphasis on one of these items. Self-centered decision-makers think only about themselves and how they will look when the situation is resolved. People-centered decision-makers do not do anything that will impose upon, or hurt others. They would rather not get a task accomplished, than risk upsetting someone.   Thing-centered decision-makers focus upon the goal to be accomplished and drive toward it, ignoring all concerns for people.

While this one-sided way of making decisions may work for an individual solving an independent problem, it does not work for a supervisor who is trying to lead a group of people.

People-centered supervisors tend to become overly concerned for the well-being of their staff. Instead of assigning a difficult task to an employee, they do the task themselves.   They resist correcting an employee's mistakes for fear of upsetting the employee.

Thing-centered supervisors become overly concerned with each task being completed exactly as they envision it. They issue instructions in minute detail and then become explosively angry if the completed project is not exactly as they wished. They tend to jump to conclusions, and shout frequently at their staff.

Self-centered supervisors only consider their own status and their own enjoyment. They take credit for successful projects, and blame their employees for failures.

Many employees who are viewed as bad are actually just responding in a predictable pattern to the treatment that they have received from their supervisors. Employees of people-centered, or **sensitive supervisors** tend to come to work late and leave early. Since their supervisor is inclined to do their work for them, they often begin to assign tasks to their supervisor.

Employees of thing-centered, or **belligerent supervisors**, begin to ignore their supervisor, especially when the supervisor is shouting.

Employees of self-centered, or **regal supervisors**, respond either by challenging the supervisor, or by refusing to do work assigned by the supervisor.

In order to become a good leader, the supervisor must begin to tame their inclination to make lop-sided decisions. The sensitive supervisor has to begin to accept that some of their actions may cause staff members to be put out, and even to not like their supervisor. They have to correct their employees' mistakes as quickly as possible, make firm decisions, and stick by them. They need to start thinking more about the success of the end product, and a little less about the employees' feelings along the way.

The belligerent supervisor has to stop and think before they speak. Instead of directing the employee to do each step of an assignment as the supervisor envisions it, they must explain the end goal and allow the employee some freedom to get there on their own. They have to consider their words by thinking more about the people involved, and their feelings, than about the exact process. They also have to accept that each project will not end up exactly as if they had done it themselves.

The regal supervisor has to begin to think about people and the products that they are to produce. They have to notice when their actions hurt their employees, and when their actions stop work from being accomplished.

The **tamed supervisor** is one who selflessly makes decisions while taking into equal consideration the people involved and the product to be produced. Once a supervisor has successfully tamed their bad traits, they will find that the great majority of their management problems have been solved. On occasion, however, in spite of all of the good communication possible, in spite of the perfect balance of selflessly considering people and things while making decisions, projects fail. This book will explore why this happens.

CHAPTER 1...CAN YOU SEE THE REAL STORY?

A Story About Hank the Dog

Hank is a very friendly Boxer. He dearly loves his family. He also dearly loves anyone who happens to be in the house at any given moment. One of Hank's favorite pastime activities is to sit beside Rachel when she is eating. As Hank sits beside Rachel, he watches the floor. He has to watch a large area of the floor because all that he knows is that at times, when Rachel eats, food pops up from the floor in a radius of about 3 feet. He is a little jumpy while he is thus engaged, because he has to be very tense and alert. He never knows when the food will pop up, and he needs to get it quickly, before any person or any other dog sees it.

If Hank were just a little smarter, he would look up, and discover that the food does not, in fact, come up from the floor, but rather drops down from the fork that Rachel is holding. If he were even smarter, he would begin to detect what type of food Rachel is eating. He might begin to correlate the fact that she drops popcorn more frequently than lasagna. If Hank could look up and see what was happening, he would be able to calmly sit beside Rachel as she eats. He would see some food miss her mouth and be able to jump to catch it. He might know that she is eating lasagna on a particular day and decide to not even bother to sit beside her, but rather to take a nap.

Observation: Sometimes We Need to Look Up

There are many things that we have learned about nature and people that we have simply accepted and never questioned. Just as Hank accepts that food pops up from the floor, we accept that certain things will happen as we have been told they will.

Sometimes it is a good idea to question these "truths", to see if they are actually as we believe. If Hank questioned where the food was coming from, he would have an easier life. If we begin to "look up" in the same manner, our lives might become correspondingly easier.

Here is an example of two things that you probably "know" and have never bothered to verify:

- The sun is directly overhead at noon each day.

- The moon is up only at night.

Now here are observations that can be verified, along with some pictures to explain it.

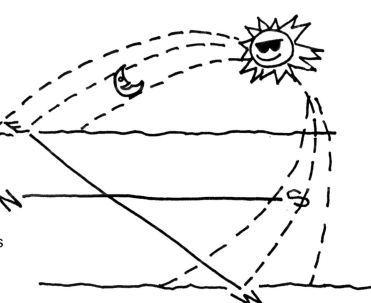

- The sun is never directly overhead unless you are at the equator. You will have to run outside the next sunny noon to see that this is true.

- The moon is up sometimes during the daytime and sometimes at night. When you think about this, you are probably already remembering that you see a faint moon up some days.

These things about the sun and the moon that you took to be true were not. There are many things about people and their behavior at work that we all believe to be true, but have never verified. I am now going to tell you a story about Harold's staff.

CHAPTER 2...PEOPLE PERFORM AT DIFFERENT LEVELS

A Story About Harold's Office

Harold supervised a group of 12 people. In the past year he had hired three new staff members: Brent, Jim, and Loren.

Brent was a pleasant person. He had graduated from a fine college, but not one that was high-powered. He had done average work in college, and did average work for Harold. Sometimes Harold was frustrated that Brent did not seem to have any original ideas, although he did the work asked of him. During the first few months of Brent's employment, Harold had needed to teach Brent some scientific concepts that he had thought Brent would have learned in college. Brent seemed to have problems with both written and spoken grammar. Harold felt that Brent was improving a bit lately, and in spite of the little problems, Brent was a consistent producer.

Jim had graduated from a high-powered college. He was confident almost to the point of arrogance. Harold was continually surprised by Jim's ideas, and the depth of Jim's knowledge. Jim always had a different way to do things. Sometimes Harold tired of all of Jim's new ideas.

Loren was probably the best employee that Harold had ever hired. He seemed to always be helpful, willing to take on almost any project. He had completed most of a 2-year degree from a community college, but seemed at times to be able to do the job of a scientist.

Harold kept thinking about Brent's slowness. He could not understand why Brent was not more like Jim. He did seem to be calmer than Jim, but Harold still wished that Brent had more drive.

Observation: There Really Are Performance "Tracks"

The last time that most of us had a chance to objectively evaluate our performance relative to others was in school. Most of us remember that in Reading class, the teacher usually broke the entire class into three smaller groups.

One group, with a name associated with red, like the Red Birds, was made up of the students who were diligent at learning to read. They mastered the reading text before the year was out. The next group had a name associated with blue. It was made up of pretty friendly students. They learned to read, but at a slower pace, and without the drive that the first group had. The last group had a name associated with yellow. This group was made up of the more rowdy students. They seemed to have an attitude that it really didn't matter much if they learned to read or not. They liked to find ways to irritate the teacher, and they generally did not seem to do their homework.

When we look at the adult population, realistically, we can see that not much changed when the school children graduated and got full-time jobs. Some people work with incredible drive, not giving up until their task is accomplished, like Jim in the story. Others happily work at sort of an average level. They will get the work done, but it may take several passes, like Brent in the story. Still others do little, if any real work.

When interviewing and hiring, it is very difficult to find out which "performance track" a candidate belongs to. Thus, an average staff will be composed of the full spectrum of work attitudes.

The supervisor has to weed out those people who do not want to work, and then assign work to fit the dedication levels of those who do want to work. A complex new job, for instance, would be assigned to a person more like Jim in the story. Brent, on the other hand, may be very happy doing a repetitive job that Jim would quickly become frustrated with. At this point, Harold does not have any apparent problems with his staff, since everyone wants to work.

More of the Story About Harold's New People

Harold had tried to organize his people into teams of equals, without team leaders. He had read about team management in a book, and it sounded like a very good idea. He was a little frustrated by the experiment. The first project that the team worked on seemed to go well, but lately he felt that they were complaining about one another, and were working more individually again. In fact, it seemed like Jim was doing most of the work for his team. Most disturbing, Loren and Jim always seemed to be complaining about one another.

At least Loren was trying to solve his problems with Jim. Harold felt silly even thinking about such personality conflicts, as he felt that people should have learned to get along with one another when they were children. He should not have to deal with such problems with adults. It seemed to Harold that at least once a week he had to tell Jim to, "Try to get along with Loren".

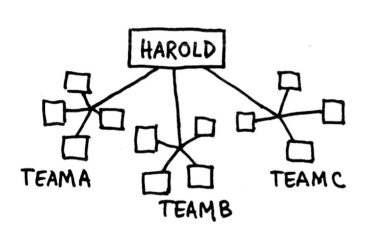

TEAM A   TEAM B   TEAM C

Observation: People Do Not Work Well in Groups Without Leaders

Working people getting along with one another and performing in group situations can also be compared to school experiences. Everyone had group projects to do in school. The projects went the same way almost every time. The teacher chose the groups, making each a cross-section of work attitudes. Someone became the leader and did most of the work. Others helped, and at least one member of the group did no work at all. The group was usually given one grade, and the person who worked the hardest always ended up angry with the person who did no work at all.

This is not much different from the work world. Teams of employees perform in about the same way that they did while in group projects in school. Some supervisors spend a good deal of time fruitlessly trying to make the team perform better than a school group.

More of the Story About Harold's Office

Harold decided not to have teams anymore. He would let each person work individually, and he would coordinate all of their work. That was his old system, and it had worked well for him. He announced his plan at a staff meeting, and was happy with it. He remembered that the office had been a nice calm place a year ago. The staff was friendly and hard-working. He had liked going to work. In the past year, however, the office had become a place that he didn't want to be. Various staff members were always angry. Things seemed to always be missing, like files, cameras, computers, and computer software. They would get lost and then turn up in odd places. Ordered supplies were late in arriving, and

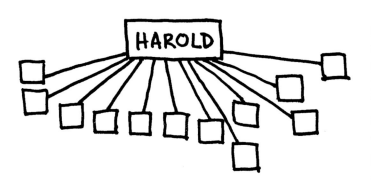

Harold often had to come up with quick, temporary replacements for the missing items.

Some projects, no matter what Harold did, seemed destined for failure. His department had lost a lot of money recently with a job that was finished late.

Harold spent a lot of time trying to head off the problems by creating new procedures. Last month, he put up a large calendar in the file room with all of the company's deadlines marked in red. This had helped the staff keep focused and helped them prioritize their work better. But, just as a new system began to work, another crisis would pop up. Harold seemed to be coming up with a new system to head off a new crisis every other week. This week, he decided that the staff needed to improve their interpersonal skills. He planned training sessions where they could learn how to get along better with each other.

Harold began to wonder if he just expected too much from his staff. Maybe he was trying too hard for perfection, and what he had was good enough. Maybe his job was to solve the crises, and he just had to accept that. He decided to talk to Loren about it the next time he saw him. Loren always had some insight to share.

CHAPTER 3...A KEY PLAYER APPEARS

A Story About Harold's Employee, Loren

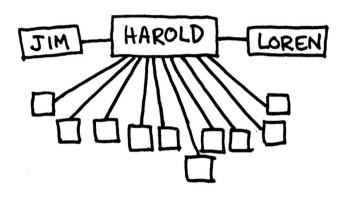

Loren was just a nice person. He was easy to talk to, and got along well with everyone. He was out-going, smiling, and a real participator in meetings. When Harold first interviewed him, he was very impressed by Loren. Loren was not shy and nervous as some people were. He laughed, he was serious, and he had an easy answer for every question. He told Harold that he was well-organized. He told Harold that he would try very hard to do a good job. Loren explained that he had actually taken four years to nearly get his Associate's Degree. Loren explained that he had training in many areas, some of which related to the work done in Harold's department. Near to the end of the interview, Loren chatted with Harold a little about Harold's children. Harold had never met a person who was so animated and easy to talk to in an interview. He had a very secure feeling when he hired Loren.

Loren seemed to be everywhere all of the time. He was the first one in each morning, and if a problem occurred at the office, he offered to stay late and help. Harold was pleased that he had hired Loren. Harold liked to talk with him. If he started to talk about a pet peeve of his with Loren, Loren listened and contributed, supporting and agreeing with Harold's position. After the talk, Harold would think, "I talked too long to Loren, but it is nice to talk to someone who thinks the way that I do".

It was only natural that Loren would take over some of Harold's tasks. He had phone calls directed away from Harold to him. In addition, he started to take care of some of the office filing, and computer backup. He even started to handle some money issues in the office. Loren started each day by distributing the mail

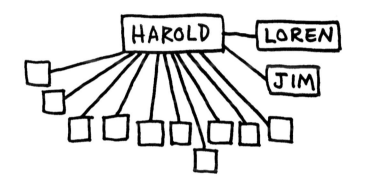

and all of the overnight faxes. He attended every meeting where he sat close to Harold. He was active in the meetings, always supporting Harold's positions. Loren had a ready laugh, and always seemed to appreciate Harold's jokes. The only problem that Harold had was that at times Loren was too active; he actually started to direct some staff members, and make some decisions that Harold should have made. Harold talked to Loren about this, and Loren backed down.

Harold found that when he talked to Loren he shared more personal information about himself than he did with others. At times he was embarrassed during meetings when Loren would make a joke about something Harold had told him. One day when discussing a piece of heavy equipment that broke Loren said, "That's just like what you were telling me about your wife's car!" Harold tried to stop telling Loren these things, but it was so easy to discuss things with him.

Loren gave Harold a birthday gift. Harold was not sure if this was appropriate or not. He tried to quickly get the gift to his car so that no one else in the office would see it.

While Loren was very active and very vocal in most situations, at times he became silent. Harold was surprised one day when he and a few members of the staff got into a very technical discussion and he called Loren into the room. Loren sat quietly, never saying a word.

Loren had some health problems, but one could not classify him as a whiner. Some days he could barely speak, yet he was at work. Often, Loren broke out into a coughing fit during meetings. Harold would offer him water, but Loren always valiantly refused.

Loren came into work one Monday morning proclaiming that he had been throwing up every 20 minutes. During the morning, about every half-hour Loren ran to the rest room. Passers-by heard loud retching sounds emanating from the rest room. Harold suggested that Loren go home, but he said, "No, I need to get this project done, I can still work." Lunchtime came and it was Loren's turn to run for sandwiches. He said, "I think that I can make it, I'll just go to the corner restaurant". The rest of the staff members were a little worried; they were not sure if they wanted to have Loren handling their food.

Loren returned with the sandwiches and distributed them to everyone. He said that he was too ill to eat. Loren left that evening saying that he would stop in at his doctor's on the way home. The next day Loren called in sick; he told Harold that his doctor said he had irritable bowel disease. The project that Loren had been working on was due, so Harold had to assign it to Jim. Jim reported that the papers were all disorganized, and that the project didn't seem to be very far along. Jim had to start the project over from scratch. Harold explained that Loren had his own system of organization, but he was sure that he could have gotten it done, if only he had not become so ill. When Loren came back to work, he was chipper, looking none the worse for the illness.

Some days when Loren came to work, it looked like a thundercloud was over his head. On other days, he was so happy that it seemed that no one could be happier. People in the office noted his moods and at times were heard saying, "Stay away from Loren, it's one of THOSE days". Harold admonished them when he heard this, noting that everyone had mood problems at times. Harold knew that he could be moody himself, at times.

One day Loren came to Harold and told him that it seemed like most of the staff was talking about Loren behind Loren's back. Harold explained to him that he was moving up in the organization, and most likely some of them were jealous. Loren seemed to perk right up after that.

Another thing that Harold liked about Loren was that he was so tactful. Loren came to him one day and told him that Jim did not seem to be performing well. Harold had not noticed this. Then for many weeks Loren told him of Jim's problem performance. Harold had not known, for instance, that Jim "had a mouth on him." Harold decided that this must mean than Jim swore a lot. He did not know that Jim had trouble doing calculations, and Loren had to help him. Loren also told Harold how he had to help Jim to get the computer to print. Now Harold could see some of Jim's problems. One day he came into the office and Jim was standing near the printer, waiting for Loren to print the pages. Loren had a little smirk on his face. Harold began to consider what to do with Jim. He would need to restrict the work that was assigned to Jim, make it a bit simpler too. Loren told Harold that he was getting tired of Jim's attitude. Harold was not sure what that meant, but he was concerned about Jim.

Loren handled problems with vendors so well. He would report how he was kept on hold on the telephone for hours with vendors and how he still solved the problem. The world was changing, and Harold had to accept that some of the company's faithful old vendors were changing too. Loren told him that they made appointments and then didn't show up. He explained how they sent the wrong merchandise, he had to send it back, and how they overcharged the company. Harold had to tell Loren to find new vendors for some of the products. Some of the replaced vendors wrote Harold letters or tried to call him, but he directed

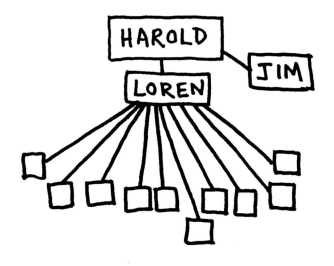

these exchanges to Loren, after all he was the one who was supposed to deal with them. Loren would become very irritated when he discovered that the vendors were trying to "get around him". He was worried that they were telling Harold bad things about him. Harold would assure him that he was not listening to them.

The company decided to do some remodeling in Harold's department. The first change was to put nameplates on the office doors. Loren came to Harold very bothered. "I'm just not comfortable with my name plate having smaller lettering than Jim's". Harold explained that project managers got slightly larger nameplates, but that it made no real difference. Loren was very unhappy, and it turned into one of his thundercloud days. Harold was uncomfortable being in the room with Loren, so he stayed in his own office all day.

Loren was promoted to the position of Office Supervisor. Within 6 months, several members of the staff resigned. Harold was surprised at the turnover. The staff members gave no reason for quitting, and Harold thought that maybe they had gotten better job offers elsewhere. Loren got worried about the turnover and asked Harold "Do you think it is because of me? I am making them come to work on time, maybe that made them angry". Harold assured him that the staff had always been required to come to work on time. Harold even pointed out to Loren that Brent had resigned and he was not even on Loren's staff.

Harold noticed that the office staff seemed to not have much work to do, and they were often sitting around talking. One had begun to bring in needlework to do. Yet the filing was not done, and supplies were needed. Harold asked Loren about this, and he explained that these people were not very smart, and that he had to assign them small bits of work to do at a time, and then watch them. "I can't let Sally file anymore. She made a real mess of it. I'll just have to do it myself after work". Harold said that it did not seem to be a good solution, but Loren smiled and said, "I don't mind". Staff members came to Harold and complained that they did not seem to be able to get any office supplies, that the filing was never done, and that their computers were not working correctly. Harold explained that Loren had problem staff members. Harold said that he and Loren were working on it. The complainers grumbled and left.

Various staff members began ordering their own supplies. They began to do their own filing, and handled other tasks that were Loren's. Harold was somewhat relieved, because this stopped much of the conflict. When the staff members ordered their own supplies, the supplies came on time. If a staff member would comment that they had been successful with getting something done that was usually Loren's responsibility, Loren would become very serious and stomp around the office for hours. Harold told them to try not to offend Loren. Loren worked very hard. He always seemed to be bustling around, but if he was stopped and asked to do more, he would always say "No problem".

Loren did have a few bad habits. Harold did not want to confront him with them, because whenever he confronted Loren, it made him so upset that he would have one of his thundercloud days. Harold decided that if Loren had these bad habits, then others probably had the same bad habits. So Harold could just make up some office policies to handle them, without confronting Loren directly. The new policies were much like those in other offices. Eating was now allowed only in the break room, because Loren was often working near documents with large sloppy sandwiches opened up. Loren even left the remains of the

sandwiches on the desk for up to a week. Coats had to be hung in the coatroom, because Loren left his lying on office furniture, sometimes not taking them home or picking them up for days. No files could go home, because Loren had started taking files home, and then they could not be used until the next day when Loren brought them back. Lunchtime could only be an hour long, because Loren tended to take much longer, especially if he went out with other staff members. No long telephone conversations were permitted, because Loren seemed to consume large amounts of time on the telephone. These were reasonable rules, and Harold thought that he should have made them before. In spite of Loren's bad habits, Harold still felt lucky to have Loren. Sometimes a vendor would be talking to Harold and would tell him how nice Loren was. "He is always so friendly and professional on the telephone", they would say.

As a further part of the remodeling, there were to be ceiling fans installed in the office. Loren volunteered to "run the job". Harold said that he thought the job would be fairly simple. They would look over the various ceiling fan styles, choose one, and have their regular electrical contractor install them. Loren said, "All I can see is a morass of problems, I just hope that we can get through it." Harold protested that it really was a simple job, but Loren was not reassured.

Loren brought in brochures from several contractors. He said he had talked to all of the contractors, some sounded good, and other sounded bad. Harold was a bit surprised, as he had not asked Loren to spend time finding a new contractor, and by the looks of the volume of literature, Loren had spent quite a bit of time. Harold said that he would rather that they use the same electrical contractor who did all of the wiring for the building. He explained that these people already knew quite a bit about the building, and that everyone was pleased with the work they had done before. Loren replied, "Ok, I just thought you might want to look at some others." He seemed to be in a bit of a huff, and Harold decided to avoid talking to Loren for a while.

Harold asked that Loren coordinate a meeting with the contractor, Loren, and himself. Loren came back to Harold and said that he had called the regular electrical contractor, and that they would not be available for 6 months. Harold sighed and told Loren to choose one from his list, then. Harold decided that perhaps it was a good thing that Loren had spent so much time locating other contractors. At the meeting, Loren sat quietly. Near to the end, when Harold had chosen the fans that he wanted to use, Loren said, "Those are much too expensive through the contractor. I have priced them much lower with other dealers, let me buy them directly." The electrical contractor was a bit worried, but said "Ok, if you can get them for less, do it. We will be coming in two weeks to put them in. We'll bring the wiring, you provide the fans." Loren said, "No problem." Harold thought, "Loren sure is sharp!" The next day Loren told Harold that he had ordered the fans. A week later, when Harold checked again, Loren said that they were making up the order and would ship in the middle of the week. The day of installation arrived and the electrical contractor showed up, but the fans were not there. Loren said, "They came, but they were the wrong ones and I sent them back. Now they are saying that it will be at least another two weeks." Harold was a little embarrassed, since he had to send the contractor away. Harold checked with Loren in one week and he said "They are having problems with the motors at the factory, it will be delayed another week." In the meantime, for some reason, the contractor called Harold. Harold was busy, so he had Loren take the call. After the call, Loren came into Harold's office and said "You won't believe this, but the contractor is withdrawing from the job! They will deliver the wire, and they want to charge us for it. I think we should force them to install the fans anyway, since they said they would." Harold sighed; another vendor gone bad. Why couldn't they just wait for the fans? It was no one's fault. Harold told Loren to make up a summary of the contractor's charges, and Loren's own notes so that he could look at the problem.

Loren said that he could direct the maintenance person, Brian, to do the wiring and install the fans. They didn't need a contractor anyway. Finally, six weeks after they were supposed to arrive, the fans came. Loren told Harold that Brian was starting to work, but he was not doing a safe job, so Loren stopped him. "What a headache" thought Harold, "I'm so glad that Loren is dealing with this." Harold also remembered that Loren said it would be a job with a lot of problems; he sure was right. Brian came to complain to Harold. "Those fans are wrong for this application, and they cost too much." Harold sighed, "Brian, please try to get along better with Loren, he knows what he is doing." Loren told Harold that he was having problems with Brian saying, "He doesn't show me any respect." Harold suggested some supervising techniques for Loren to try. Finally, Brian said that he was too busy to work on the fans any more.

Loren tried to install the fans himself with the help of Clara, the accountant. The wiring for the first fan had been completed before Brian became too busy. Loren told Harold that they would start at 8 AM the next morning. At 10 AM the next day Harold saw Loren and asked, "Are the fans all up?" Loren replied with a sigh "No, we haven't gotten started. There were computer problems that I had to deal with first." By the end of the day, they had gotten one fan up. "What a dedicated employee!" Harold thought. But, he was a little confused about how long it took Loren to put up the fans. He was pretty sure that it was a job that should have taken

an hour or two, and it took Loren all day. He decided that these must be more complicated fans than he was aware of. He told Loren to wait until the maintenance people were free, because he should not have to install fans with everything else that he was doing.

One day a few weeks later, Harold almost asked Loren about the fans. They were standing near to where the fans were in their boxes, and he said "About the fans…" and saw Loren's face begin to tighten up. He decided that he would rather not have the fans today, when Loren still had to finish getting a report out. The fans never got installed.

These fans were just one element in the "mini-crisis" problem that Harold was thinking about. It seemed like some projects in the office got done, and some never got done. Loren thought that the problem was with the employees and the vendors. Loren had certainly tried everything he could with his employees. He had met with each employee individually and talked over their work problems. Loren felt that this helped. "Maybe they just need more of my attention," he said. "I try to be always available for them."

One of the problems that some of Loren's staff told Loren about was their lack of ability to contact Loren at times. Loren was mystified. Any time that he was away from the office he had his pager on, and his staff had his home number. He knew that he was home all day once when he was sick, yet his staff said that they had not been able to reach him. He told Harold about the problem, and Harold just added it to his mini-crisis list. As they talked about the office problems, Loren became concerned that perhaps he was a bad supervisor, and he asked Harold what he thought. Harold said "No, of course not." Loren was a good supervisor; he was just

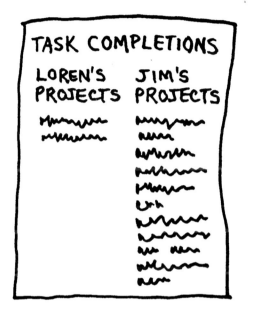

TASK COMPLETIONS

LOREN'S PROJECTS   JIM'S PROJECTS

the victim of circumstances. "You certainly treat your people well, and you have the patience of a saint", Harold told Loren. Loren also reminded Harold that Jim was still a bit of a problem, "Maybe the staff has a bad attitude because of Jim", Loren said.

Sometimes it seemed to Harold that so little was accomplished with Loren's staff that he could not honestly say what Loren actually did. Once, when he sat down and made a list of everything that Loren did, it was not very long. He figured that since Loren was always busy, it must be that Harold just didn't understand the details that Loren worked on. Then, the very next day, Loren arrived with a pile of completed work, his staff was working industriously, and Harold had to admit that Loren seemed to have a model team. Harold decided that he was wrong, and Loren was working hard.

Since Loren was trying so hard to handle his difficult staff, Harold decided that maybe a supervisor training course would help. He found one, and told Loren about it. Loren was very pleased when he saw that it was being offered in Florida. For several days before the training, Loren mentioned it in each conversation that he had with others in the office. When he returned from the training Harold asked him how it had gone. Loren spent a good hour telling Harold how silly and useless it was. Harold felt that he had not picked a good course.

CHAPTER 4...THE KEY PLAYER SEEN BY OTHERS

Loren, From His Staff's Perspective

Clara had worked in the office for four years before Loren came. She was the accountant for the company and enjoyed her work with numbers. After about 6 months at his new job, Loren took over supervision of Clara, along with the entire office support staff. Clara thought that Loren was a nice person, and enjoyed the fact that Loren took her out to lunch right after he was made a supervisor. No other supervisor had taken Clara out to lunch.

Loren had monthly staff meetings. Clara attended, but didn't think that much of the meeting would matter to her since she had been doing the same job for four years. Loren had Clara list her tasks, and then after a month or so, Loren took over some of Clara's tasks himself, mostly those having to do with purchasing. Clara didn't like the meetings much. Loren always came in late, and sighed, explaining that Harold had a last minute problem which Loren had to help with. Loren always asked the same questions, that were answered in the same way. Loren seemed to use a different tone of voice for the meetings, sort of a sighing singsong voice. It sounded like he thought that he was very superior to them all.

The time that Loren became so violently ill and came to work anyway, Clara noticed that as he distributed the sandwiches to the employees, one more large sandwich was in the bottom of the bag. Later, Clara noticed that Loren has hunched over his desk and seemed to be eating. Alice and Clara talked about it. "I'm pretty sure that he was eating" Clara concluded. When he returned from his sick day, Loren told Clara that he had food poisoning. He said

"I'm glad that's over, I haven't eaten anything in three days". Clara thought that this was odd since she had seen him eating the large sandwich, just two days ago.

The day that Loren was at home, he told his staff that they should call him if they had any questions. Clara called and called, but could not reach Loren. Jim wanted Clara to order a piece of equipment. Since Clara could not get any direction from Loren, and she had done such an order before, Clara started to do it for Jim. When Loren returned, he was so incensed that he began to yell, "I told you to call me at home! If Harold saw you doing this he would blow up!" Clara tried to protest, and to explain but to no avail. Loren took the work from Clara and disappeared into his office.

Clara resolved never to do anything unless Loren said it was on her task list. Clara began to talk to other staff members about Loren. Jim especially had problems with Loren. Mostly they said things to each other like "Watch out today, he's on the warpath".

Jim became frustrated when Clara told him that she hadn't ordered his equipment. He saw Harold in the hallway and said, "I'm having trouble getting my equipment". Harold strode to Clara's desk and asked her about it. Clara replied, "I don't know where the equipment is, Loren had the ordering papers last." As soon as Harold left, Loren took Clara aside and yelled at her, "Don't ever make me look bad in front of Harold again." Clara was a little shocked, but didn't say anything. More and more she was trying to figure out what to say to Loren; it seemed that no matter what happened, Loren yelled at her. It all seemed so irrational.

Loren got busier and busier. He often canceled the monthly staff meetings; things were just too busy to sit down and talk with the staff.

Clara answered a telephone call from the regular electrical contractor. He said, "I hear that Harold wants some fans, just tell me when he wants them". Clara explained that Loren was overseeing the project but that he was busy at the moment. Clara gave Loren the message to call the contractor. She noted that Loren didn't call him back right away, he just took the message and added it to his paper pile.

Jim was very angry and said, "Where is my equipment, Clara?" Clara reminded him that Loren had the paperwork. Jim grumbled and ordered the equipment himself.

Clara almost could not bear hearing Loren talking with Harold. Loren laughed much too loudly at Harold's jokes. Clara heard Loren claim that he had done things that Clara herself had done. Clara saw a paper one day that was re-copied in Loren's handwriting, but Clara had done all the work. Clara was sure that Harold saw all of these things, so she just waited to see what he would do.

A few staff members quit. "I can't take Mr. Perfect anymore, I'll go somewhere were I get credit for my own work," they said.

Clara was surprised when she was asked to help install the fans, and she was a little irritated. Why did she have to install fans when there were other people who could do it? Nevertheless, she was ready to go at 8 AM, but Loren was nowhere to be seen. Clara didn't want to wait and wait, so she found the pieces of the fans and the instructions, and she started to assemble them. By the time that Loren arrived at a little after 10 AM, Clara had three of the fans assembled and ready to go. Loren began to yell, "I told you to wait for me, you don't know enough about this to do this yourself!" Clara stopped and went to get a cup of coffee. The other staff members

teased her. "Special electrical assistant to Loren today?" From then on, the project consisted of Loren re-assembling the fans with Clara handing him tools. By 5 PM, they had gotten one fan up. A few days later Clara asked Loren "Aren't we going to install the rest of the fans?" "No", Loren replied, "Harold decided that he didn't want them anymore."

Clara began to think about getting a new job. With everyone talking about Loren, and Loren angry with everyone, it had turned into an unfriendly office to be in. But Clara liked Harold, so she stuck with it. She was sure that Harold could see how nasty Loren was, and she was sure that Harold would fix the problem.

Loren, From His Co-worker's Perspective

Jim could not believe that Harold kept Loren around. He asked Loren about the order for his equipment and Loren said that he was not involved in that. Later in the day Loren brought the paperwork to Jim. He explained that Harold thought that it was too expensive, so Loren would need to get three quotes. Jim often noted that Loren's stories changed from moment to moment. Jim had seen Loren tell outright lies. One time the staff was looking for a particular file, and Loren said it was in the cabinet with the rest of the project, he had filed it there himself. Later in the day Jim saw Loren duck into his own office, and come out with the file and place it on the table in the file room.

Jim saw that Loren always laughed at Harold's jokes, and even gave him gifts. Jim felt like Loren was trying to make him look bad. Jim's spouse told him that he was getting to be paranoid. Whenever Jim absolutely had to get something done, and Loren was working with him, it seemed that Loren was unable to deliver some vital part of the project. Take this equipment, for instance. Jim had ordered similar things many times before and it had been a simple process. Now the order had waited a few weeks and it looked like the process was going to take even longer. Because Loren had control of it, it had to wait for three quotes. Jim finally decided to just order it himself.

When the equipment arrived Harold said, "I'm glad that is finally here. What took so long?" Jim felt that Loren was the cause of the problem, but he felt strongly that it was improper to tattle, and he was sure that Harold knew what the problem was. So he just responded "I don't know." Loren got his straight mouth look and stomped out of the room.

Jim was also frustrated with the computers. They used to work, and now it seemed like whenever he sat down at one, it had something wrong with it. He had to get Loren to help him, just to get documents printed. Loren had a little triumphant look on his face when the document came out. "See how easy it is when you let me help?" he asked. Jim said nothing.

Brian, the maintenance man, asked Loren for some specifications for the fans that he was supposed to install. Loren said that there were none. Brian attempted to draw up a wiring plan and showed it to Harold. Loren saw them talking and joined them. Harold asked if there were any fan specifications, and Loren produced them. Brian asked Loren about the specifications after the impromptu meeting. Loren said, "Oh, I didn't know that those were what you wanted." When Brian started to work on the fans, Loren came out and said, "You need high-voltage electrical gloves to do that work." Brian explained that the power was turned off and locked out, and that this was just a normal electrical wiring project, and he did not need gloves. But he didn't want to deal with the fans

and Loren any more, so he told Loren that he was too busy to finish the job.

Jim began to watch Loren more carefully. He noted that Loren seemed to always be in motion. He officiously walked from work area to work area, often carrying papers. Sometimes Loren sighed and riffled through the papers that he was carrying. He called people and left messages. What Jim seldom saw Loren do was any actual work. He began to think about the things missing in the file room and the fact that whenever Loren was asked for them, he did not seem to go to the file room. Jim was not sure where Loren went, but after about 20 minutes Loren would arrive with the needed paper. When Jim asked where he had found it, Loren would always say, "It was right there on the shelf". One day, Jim asked Loren for a file and said "I'll follow you so that you can show me where these things are kept." Loren became very agitated, and couldn't find the file. About a half hour later he appeared at Jim's side, saying, "I found it, it was caught behind the other files". Jim thought that this was unlikely, but he had no better explanation.

Jim thought that oddest of all were large things that seemed to disappear and then re-appear. Several laptop computers were missing. Jim got frustrated because this made work slow down while everyone scrambled to find backup data for what had been on the computers. Harold said that they should all be patient, that these things always turned up. A few weeks later the laptop computers were found on the table in the break room. Jim began to keep his equipment locked in his desk. It got so that he could not stand the sight of Loren, so Jim started to work in his office with the door closed.

Brent found that Loren was very helpful to him right after he was hired. Whenever he was trying to figure out what he was

supposed to do next, Loren would pop up at his side and tell him what Harold wanted him to do. When Loren was promoted to be in charge of the office support staff, he told Brent that now Brent would be reporting to him, along with the office staff. Brent said that he thought project managers still reported to Harold, but Loren said," no, I am Harold's assistant so the entire office now reports to me." Brent found the directions from Loren to be more and more confusing.

Everyone in the coffee room talked about their annoyances with Loren all of the time. "Did you notice how Loren wears the same types of ties as Harold?" Clara observed. Jim said "Yes, and how about how he wears only green casual shirts on Fridays, just like Harold." "What I hate", Brian said, "is the way that Loren comes in the door carrying his briefcase in the same manner that Harold does, and then says his good mornings in the same manner as Harold also. Doesn't he have a life of his own?"

Brent found the coffee room gossip to be unpleasant also, so he decided to look for another job that didn't involve Loren. Brent resigned as soon as he had found a new job.

Loren, From Contractors' Perspectives

The old electrical contractor had worked for the company for years before Loren arrived. They had always been helpful, honest, and economical. Harold called to say that he wanted to install fans. They called back three times. Twice they left a message for Loren to call them. Finally they reached Loren. He said to them "We are putting that project on hold for awhile."

The new electrical contractor was happy to do the job. After the first meeting they were a little displeased at only being able to install the fans and provide the wire. They liked it better when they could ensure the quality of the entire product. They also knew that they could get the fans cheaper than Loren said he could. They could not understand what he was saying because their proposal specifically detailed the cost of the fans, and it was less than Loren stated. Nonetheless, they wanted to "break in" to work for Harold's department. They figured that Harold must have seen the cost difference in the proposal and wanted it this way, so they agreed.

As they were preparing to do the job, Loren called the contractor and asked for a change in the size of wire going to the fans. Loren said that they did not need a ground wire. The contractor argued that they could not make that change. They could not understand why an office manager would even care about the type of wire that they planned to use. Wasn't the contractor supposed to know the materials, and wiring rules, better? Loren then demanded a more detailed schedule of costs. The contractor provided the new cost schedule, but began to be upset at the extra work that they were being forced to provide for the job. Loren called them, demanded the wire without the ground, and said that the cost was still too high. He yelled, "You have to do it my way. You are the contractor and are not hired to think, but to do as I say." He went on to say "If you bring cable with a ground wire in it, I will withhold payment from you." When they refused to do the project unsafely, Loren said he would get someone else to do the wiring, but they could still come and bolt up the fans. The contractor called Harold who said, "Loren is helping to coordinate this, he knows what I want." The contractor protested that Loren was making the system unsafe. Harold asked the contractor to "Try to get along with Loren." The second time that the contractor called Harold, he refused to talk to them. Finally the contractor had to refuse to do the work. Loren called them and yelled at them for failing to provide the product that they promised. When they again protested that the product as he had defined it was unsafe, Loren replied, "You are just trying to run up the price for your own profit." They told Loren that they would deliver what they had already ordered for the project, and would have to charge for the wire and the time to deliver it. Loren informed them that "They would have no more business with the company."

Loren, From a Fan Vendor's Point of View

The fan supplier got a call from Loren at the start of the project, and they provided him with some pamphlets. Eight weeks after the first call, Loren again called and ordered some fans. He said that they had to be sent overnight. He instructed them to make up the bill without calling out the overnight charges. Loren told them to just put the cost of the fans plus the overnight charges on one line, saying, "I want the bill to say 6 fans and a total cost." The fan supplier protested that they would have to create the bill by hand, since the computer generated bills with itemization. They even explained that most people want itemized bills. Loren started to yell at them "How difficult can this be? Send me a bill that says 6 fans and a total cost!" When the vendor began to protest again Loren roared "Do you want to sell me the fans or not?" The vendor meekly complied.

Observation: Loren is the Problem

By now it is obvious that Loren presents different personalities to different people. To Harold, Loren is always helpful and is a confidant. Loren is the person always there to pull the company out of a crisis. Harold has some problems with what Loren does, but for the most part views Loren as a "right-hand man". Harold never sees or hears Loren yelling at staff members or vendors, and would be incredulous if someone said that Loren did.

To his staff, Loren is an unpredictable tyrant. He yells continually, stops them from working, and assigns work in such tiny pieces that they often have nothing to do.

To his co-workers, Loren is a liar and a cheat. They know that he does no actual work, and they suspect that he hides files and equipment. They see that he "sucks up" to Harold, and they are incredulous that Harold does nothing about it. They solve their problems by distancing themselves from Loren.

Loren is as unpredictable to contractors and to vendors as he is to his staff. At times Loren is patient, friendly and polite. At other times he yells and demands the impossible. Faithful, long term vendors feel that they are being systematically browbeaten until they leave.

Observation: There Were Cheaters in School

Returning to the school analogy, we must remember that some students did not do their homework, and lied about it. Some always copied their homework from other students. Others were sick on days when major projects were due. The cheating was obvious to the other students, but not always caught by the teachers, especially the newer teachers.

Catching cheaters in school was a sort of a game that most of us watched, but did not participate in. There was a sort of unspoken code whereby students did not turn in cheaters, they simply waited to see if the teacher was smart enough to catch on. Often the person was caught with a "pop quiz". Those who knew the material did well, those who had copied from others, thus not learning the lesson, were caught, and given a zero.

While we knew that there were cheaters in school, we also knew how adults in the work world were going to behave and specifically what they would and would not do. We knew this because we were told how they would act. We were told:

Working people never:

- Come to work late.
- Forget their tools.
- Fail to get their work done on time.
- Misspell words.
- Use bad grammar.
- Treat co-workers unfairly.
- Read their speech.
- Forget to put their names on their work.
- Lie or cheat.

While in school, the teacher was clearly in charge, and we were told that in the work world the boss would be even more in charge. "Your boss won't let you get away with that", we learned. We were told that cheaters only cheat themselves; we knew that they would be quickly found out in the work world because they would not have learned the material and skills to be successful in the job. If they even managed to get a job, they would be found out, and fired.

Observation: The Cheaters Are at Work, Too

We were told that the work world would be like school, but better. The boss would be tougher than our teacher, and cheaters would be caught. As adults we begin work prepared to watch the final end of these people.

The only hitch is that a work organization is very different from a school. A supervisor in the work world is not promoted into their position because of their leadership ability, nor are they given any leadership training. They are promoted because they have the correct education and training for the work that the company does, or because the upper management likes them. So here they are, suddenly in charge of some people who have spent at least 12 years perfecting their ability to cheat and lie and other people who have spent at least 12 years silently watching the game be played. This is a perfect environment for cheaters to thrive. The supervisors are sitting ducks.

The people who cheat and lie can have a free-for-all. They have so perfected their systems that they are virtually invisible to their supervisors. They will not be reported by their peers, who will be watching and waiting for "Management" to catch them. Since there are no pop quizzes to show that these people are not working, it is very difficult for a supervisor to even detect the problem.

Most of us use our school concepts to define what the working world is like, and to define good and bad performance in employees. We have to spend a bit of time making excuses for the cheaters who do not seem to be caught, so that they fit into our description of what we believe the world is like.

The cheaters become more sophisticated as they progress through each year, and each teacher or supervisor. The game goes on, and most of us do not know how to stop it.

CHAPTER 5...WHAT WAS THE KEY PLAYER THINKING?

A Story About Loren Getting Caught

Harold was frustrated with a repeating office computer problem. Whenever Brent tried to print out drawings, the computer brought up an error message and refused to print. Brent had tried to troubleshoot the problem, but was unsuccessful. Harold asked Loren about it and Loren replied, "I don't know what is wrong with Brent. When I print it, it comes right out. I think that Brent just does not understand computers." Loren continued with a sigh "I guess that I will just have to print out all of the drawings myself." One day Harold said, "Loren, show me what you do, then I'll try to teach Brent to do it." Loren sat down by the computer and could not get it to print out. Harold waited, then said, "This looks like the same problem that Brent had. Show me how you overcome it." Loren became very agitated. Harold became embarrassed by how upset Loren was becoming, and left the room. A half-hour later, Loren came into Harold's office with the drawing. "I forgot the last setting, but it worked fine then."

Loren was off one day, and Brent once again could not get the computer to print. Harold volunteered to help. He could not get it to print. Clara walked by and suggested "Loren always prints those from his computer in his office." Harold went to Loren's office and had no problem printing the drawing.

When Loren returned, Harold called Loren into his office. "Loren, I am pretty upset. I have a problem, it looks like you are lying".

Loren said: "OK."

Harold continued: "Maybe you are just overloaded, but this problem involves the printing of figures with the computer. You said that you could get the computer to print the figures."

Loren calmly said: "Yes."

Harold sighed: "But in fact no one can print on that computer. You yourself print with the printer in your office."

Loren said: "Yes."

Harold went on: "You implied that the problem was with Brent"

Loren: "Yes."

Harold: "That is lying. If it ever happens again, I will fire you."

Loren, still seemingly unruffled: "OK."

Harold was very confused. He had confronted Loren, and instead of giving a logical explanation, Loren had agreed that he had lied. Harold had even offered an excuse of Loren being overworked, and Loren had not used it. When Harold went home that night he talked it over with his life-mate. She suggested that Loren was actually very underconfident. "Didn't you tell me that Loren does not have a degree? He must feel that everyone compares him to the others who do have degrees. He is probably trying to cover it up and that is why it sounds like he is lying." Harold decided that Loren most likely was underconfident. He decided that the lying was most likely a one-time occurrence, because Loren was "pushed to the wall" and not able to solve the computer problem. Harold resolved to get a technician in the next day to look over the problem.

The technician said, "It was pretty simple. Somehow the printer driver was not installed." Harold laughed at the solution, and began to look for ways to increase Loren's confidence.

Observation: We Do Not Think the Same Way as These People Do

Since we all know that people who cheat and lie will not be able to succeed in the work world, we tend to dismiss any thought that people <u>are</u> really cheating and lying and succeeding at it. We instead spend a great deal of time trying to find a logical, rational explanation to dismiss our observations that these people might be lying. We try to force the events into the picture of the world that we believe. We try very hard to find excuses for them. When we catch them we help out by saying things like "I know you have been ill" or "I know that you are overworked" or "Maybe you didn't understand what I meant". Our final excuse for people who are bossy and arrogant while seeming to lie and be incompetent is that they must feel "underconfident", and that we "need to help them to fit in better".

Underconfident people are quiet; they speak with many qualifiers "I'm sure that you thought about this but…" "I think that you probably already did this but…" Underconfident people are shy people. Mousy is more a word to be used for them, rather than bossy and arrogant.

What then, are people like Loren doing? We know now that they are not working. We also know that they are lying. We can see now that they are creating situations of chaos and confusion wherever they go. They are stopping others from getting their work done. They are causing projects to fail. Why would anyone want to do that?

In his book "People of the Lie" M. Scott Peck explores people like Loren, who he calls evil people. He describes counseling a Loren-type person over the course of four years. Near to the end of the four years he asks the person:

MSP: "You used to claim [to create chaos and confusion] was accidental. Now we've learned it is often your intention to do so. But I still don't understand why it's your intention".

Loren-type: "Because it is fun"

MSP: "Fun?"

Loren-type: "Yes it's fun to confuse you. I've told you. It gives me a sense of power".

MSP: "But wouldn't it be more fun to get a sense of power out of being genuinely competent?"

Loren-type: "*I* don't think so."

MSP: "Does it bother you that you're having this fun at the expense of other people?"

Loren-type: "No. Maybe it would if I seriously hurt somebody. But I don't, do I?"

MSP: "Even though your destructiveness may be minor, it still seems to me that there's something—well, something evil about your delight in it."

Loren-type: "I suppose you could say that."

MSP: "I can't believe you." "Here I've virtually called you evil, and you don't seem the least bit upset by it."

Loren-type: "So what do you want me to do about it?"

Observation: Some People Purposely Sabotage Work, Purely for Their Own Feelings of Power and Enjoyment

These people want to have control of every situation, and to be the center of attention in it. They thrive on situations of chaos and confusion that they themselves create. They like to work with authority figures to solve the problems that they themselves created.

Loren was happy when he was dominating the office with his illness. He had no intention of actually doing the work on the project that he had to do. He instead made the entire office staff miserable with his retching. He refused to go home. Finally, when the project had to be completed, he did stay home, was unavailable, and waited until Jim completed the work. The involvement of the office staff in his illness was what he wanted.

With the fan project, Loren wanted to be the savior, after the contractors had let him down. He had to work a bit to get the contractors to let him down, but he managed it. Then he waited to start the project himself so that he would have the longest dramatic time to be seen working and sacrificing. When he had milked all of the attention that he could out of the project, he simply abandoned it.

CHAPTER 6...CAN YOU SEE THE PLAYERS?

People who cheat and lie behave in a predictable manner. Here is a list of cheater behavior, compared to one of "regular" people.

Cheaters	"Regular People"
Act illogically.	Act logically.
Are more friendly to authority figures.	Are equally friendly to everyone.
Give their supervisor gifts.	Only give gifts if it is the norm for the office.
Imitate their supervisor, dress like their supervisor.	Dress in their own style.
Are unfriendly to those who they perceive to be lower than themselves.	Are friendly to all "levels" of personnel.
Are expressive, laughing loudly, bustling authoritatively.	Are not room-dominating with their emotions.
Become ill when a major project is due.	Finish their work.
Make their entire office become involved in their ailments.	Are not obvious with their ailments.
Become very upset if their status symbols are removed.	Like status symbols, but do not become obsessed with them.
Blame others when work is not done.	Take blame themselves.
Do not actually get any work done.	Get work done.
Control communications; especially keeping others from talking to the boss.	Do not control communications.
Are promoted quickly.	Are promoted at a normal pace.
Gossip for long periods of time.	Gossip, then stop and go back to work.
Had trouble finishing higher education.	Finish their higher education on a normal schedule.
Are constantly involved in projects that fail.	Are usually involved in projects that are successful.
Ask employees and contractors to do dangerous and unethical things.	Do not ask people to do dangerous or unethical things.
Are very likeable during their interview.	Are nervous, and even stumble over their words in their interview.
Profess in their interview to be "organized" and a "quick learner".	Do not brag about their skills in an interview.
Find a strong-willed employee and make them a scapegoat.	Never use a scapegoat.
Are on hand to help solve every office crisis.	Are involved in some, but not all office crises.
Break things and have accidents more frequently than others.	Break things and have accidents at predictable rates.
Often have to work late into the night to solve a crisis.	Generally get work done on time, not often in a crisis.
Are slow at getting work started.	Start work at reasonable times.
Are silent in any discussion that requires real knowledge.	Talk about what they know.
Complain vaguely that others are, "talking behind their backs", not "treating them with respect", or "overcharging the project".	Complain about others with specific logical facts.

CHAPTER 7...AFTERMATH

A Story About Loren's Resignation

After Brent left, Loren asked Harold if he could try to work on some of Brent's projects. Harold agreed. Loren seemed capable, and had been with the company long enough to understand what they did.

Jim began to be really irritated with Loren. The final straw for him was when Harold assigned Brent's project management work to Loren. Jim went to Harold and complained, but Harold told him that Loren wanted to try the job, and it seemed harmless.

Jim began to challenge Loren more and more. He asked to watch while Loren fixed a computer program. When he heard Loren telling Harold something, Jim walked up and said "No, you are mistaken, Loren. Clara did that, I saw her working on it." He heard Loren telling everyone that the manufacturer never made a fitting in a particular size, and instead of keeping silent as before, he went to his own office, got the fitting that he was using as a paperweight, and took it out for all to see. Every time that Jim knew that Loren was lying, he pointed it out. Jim tried to stay calm and polite while doing this, but sometimes his voice got a little shaky. Sometimes he was a little rude. As he got more practice, he found that he could stay calmer, and could to stick to the point, which was just debunking Loren's lies. Jim began to think about all of the things that Loren had said and done. One day when he didn't feel well he said "Loren, who is your doctor?" Loren asked why, and Jim replied, "Because when you were so ill that time you said you were going to stop by his office on the way home, and I thought that I would like to go to a doctor that you can stop and visit with no appointment." Loren said, "Well, he has discontinued his practice now."

Jim tried to find areas where Loren might be stealing from the company. He reasoned that if Loren were lying about working, then he most likely was also stealing money. He looked over Loren's expense reports, and found nothing out of line. He watched Loren's purchases, and found nothing out of line. He was sure that Loren was probably stealing, but he could not find any documentation of it.

Loren took some of Jim's work to Harold. He had marked up Jim's project cost estimate. Loren spoke in a scoffing tone "I don't know where Jim got these numbers, I can't verify them." Harold called Jim in and asked him to verify the numbers. Jim had to work for a few hours but finally presented a large packet for Harold with a copy for Loren and for the other project managers. Each cost was detailed, each of Loren's accusations was countered. Loren's accusations looked stupid in light of so much back-up information. Harold told Jim to try to get along with Loren, and Jim replied that he was just trying to do his job.

Finally one day, Loren came to Jim and yelled, "What is wrong with you, why are you making this job run so slowly?" Jim tried to defend himself saying, "I'm not making it run slowly, I just like work to be done well, and on time". Loren attacked again, a little illogically, "But you did that terrible job with ordering the equipment." Jim thought to defend himself again, but instead decided to attack back saying, "My problem is the fact that you constantly lie and twist facts." Jim said that he didn't like the way that Loren worked. Loren asked him for specific examples and Jim gave some. For each example Loren had a rebuttal. Loren yelled, "I'm sorry if I upset you, but you are worrying about petty problems.

We have a job to do, let's try to work together." Jim lost his temper and yelled back, "I can't take your lying anymore." Loren left Jim's office and stormed into Harold's.

Loren seemed quite shaken and said to Harold "I can't take this from Jim anymore." Harold asked what happened and Loren said, "He claims that I lie." "Did you lie again?" asked Harold.

Loren was taken aback. Harold went on to explain, "You said last week that a fitting did not exist, yet Jim had one just like it in his office. That seemed like a lie to me." Loren agreed "That was a lie but" he went on to say, "all I know is that Jim has had it in for me ever since he started here, and now you are on his side." He stormed out of the office and talked to no one for the rest of the day. The next day Loren brought a resignation letter to Harold and said, "I don't want to do this, but my presence is hurting this company. Jim is more needed that I am, so I am resigning." Harold had an urge to say, "Oh, stay, its not so bad, you obviously know about the problem, and want to improve." But Harold had had many years of experience as a supervisor and knew that, as sorry as he was to see Loren go, he should just let it happen. Loren was gone.

Observation: These People Leave When Confronted

M. Scott Peck observes that: "They flee from self-examination and any situation in which they might be closely examined by others".

The evil cheating people like Loren are not generally confronted in the business setting. Everyone has years of practice watching the interplay between the cheater and the supervisor, but no practice at catching the cheater. To top it off, all of us have a very great resistance to being a tattletale. So everyone simply waits for the "teacher" to catch the cheater. Even if a supervisor has a suspicion that there is a problem, the cheater has hidden files, lost documents, and generally made it impossible for anything to "stick" on them.

Confronting them takes a strong and persistent person. This person has to be continually pointing out their lies, while resisting everyone else telling them to "try to get along" with the cheater.

Most people begin to look for the criminal things that the Loren-type person has done. But assuming criminal intent is just another way of trying to fit them back into the old system that we had accepted. They are not doing anything traditionally, documentably wrong. They are not "on the take". They are not profiting from their actions in any way. They are merely creating chaos and confusion while controlling every situation.

Since they are in control of most situations, including most of the office communication, they easily see when someone is on to them. When they suspect that they are going to be exposed, they suddenly do their work, as Loren did when Harold began to make lists of his tasks. They mount an attack on the person that they see as most dangerous to them. In this case, Loren tried to use innuendos to discredit Jim.

Whenever the Loren-type person first gets backed into a corner, they insist on having every small problem detailed one by one, so that they can refute them one by one, and show that the accuser is just petty. They then make sweeping managerial statements like "We need to coordinate more", or "We need to set goals together".

They are very skilled at subterfuge, but also know when they are found out, and will readily admit it when confronted. They are, after all, just playing a game of power and manipulation.

If the supervisor catches the Loren-person in a lie, the Loren-person will offer to resign by saying, "It is clear that I am hurting the company, I do not ever want to do that, so I will resign." This "I am hurting the company" line most often causes the supervisor to retract their statement and say, "No, you should stay, just don't do that again". The Loren-type person is happy to lie by agreeing not to lie again. The supervisor is sure that the person is sincere, just a little misdirected, and sincerely wants to improve. It is much easier for a supervisor to do this than to admit to themselves that they have been wrong.

Observation: Removing People Who Cheat Takes Persistent Exposure

The person trying to expose a cheater needs to:

- Persistently point out the inconsistencies, in group settings.
- Stick to logical facts.
- Not be rude or inflammatory.
- Document what they see, and spread the documentation around as much as possible.
- Not spend great amounts of time defending themselves, rather spend time attacking back with truths.
- Agree with the cheater that they think they are lying, if in a one-on-one situation.

The person who cheats will respond by:

- Becoming angry when they begin to lose control.
- Using illogical arguments that become more illogical as the exposure continues.
- Resigning and leaving without a trace, after they are fully exposed.

A Story About the Aftermath

Once Loren left, the office seemed to be very quiet. The staff spoke in hushed tones. Finally Harold went to the break room and started to chat about it. As the staff got warmed up to the topic they told him all about Loren from their side of the picture. Harold was horrified. He began to wonder about Loren's work. For the first few weeks, no one did Loren's job and it didn't seem to affect the operations of the company at all. In fact, things seemed to go more smoothly. Harold went to find a file, and found that many of the files in the file room were miss-labeled. With a sinking feeling, he started to look at the project that Loren was working on. Nothing had been done on it. He tripped over the box of fans, and decided to call the old electrical contractor, who told him that they had never had a call back from Loren. He asked them to come, and by the end of the week the fans were up. The copier was repaired; Sally went into the file room and organized the files. The office slowly became a neat and orderly place that was nice to work in. Harold gave Loren's project to Jim.

After a few months, Harold noticed that all of the work was getting done, and no deadlines were being missed. Also, he was not solving personality problems, and the staff was working together in a way that could only be called teamwork.

CHAPTER 8...WHY PROJECTS FAIL

A project succeeds if everyone working on it shares a goal for the project to succeed. Wars are won, people land on the moon, the environment is cleaned up, millennium celebrations around the world occur without a mishap, all because everyone decides that this is what should happen. There may be problems and setbacks, but in the end the project gets done.

Projects fail when a self-centered person decides to make them fail, and there is no one strong enough or courageous enough to oppose them.

T

U

V